CEVNI

CEVNI (Code Européen des Navigation Intérieure) is a United ~~...~~ signals and standardises navigational procedures on the European ~~... oasis~~ of the regulations of various countries and commissions, such as RPNR ~~...ent~~ de Police pour la Navigation du ~~R~~hin), RGPF (Règlement Général de Police Française) and BPR (Binnenvaart Politie Reglement).

The regulations cited above are, in some aspects, more specific than CEVNI which, because it applies throughout a vast network of waterways, cannot individually address each and every situation which might arise. Nevertheless, as CEVNI covers the majority of situations, in general terms a pleasure craft master who knows and understands CEVNI will be prepared for most situations. However, on certain navigations, local conditions demand that additional signs, signals and regulations are applied, though they are not mentioned, even in general terms in CEVNI. Some of those have been incorporated into this Code.

The text of this Code sometimes refers to 'normal vessels'. This has a specific meaning in this context. CEVNI gives vessels which are 20 metres long or more priority over smaller craft, therefore, this Code refers to vessels of 20 metres or more, as 'normal vessels'. (NOTE: Some authorities may class vessels over 15 metres as normal vessels.)

Normal vessels have priority over small craft, therefore it follows that many of the regulations given in this Code do not apply to the majority of pleasure craft. Nevertheless it is essential that the master of a pleasure craft knows them. In order to navigate safely, the master of a pleasure craft must understand the intentions of normal vessels, so it is essential that he/she is able to interpret the signs and signals which may be given to, or by, those vessels.

BASIC RULES

Do not navigate if your capacity is reduced by fatigue or intoxication. Be vigilant and use good navigational practice. Avoid endangering human life, obstructing shipping, damaging banks, installations etc. Take any necessary steps to avoid imminent danger, even if that means disregarding regulations.

BOATMASTER

Someone with the necessary skill and qualifications must be in control of the boat. He/she is responsible for compliance with these regulations and must be on board when the vessel is underway, though not necessarily at the helm. From here on, this person will be referred to as the 'boatmaster' and others as the 'crew'. To ensure safe navigation and good order on board, crew must obey the boatmaster's orders and assist in complying with these regulations.

YOUR BOAT

The boat's dimensions and speed must be suitable for the waterway it is navigating. There must be enough skilled crew members to navigate and ensure the safety of those on board. When underway, the person steering must be suitably qualified and at least 16 years old, unless the authorities have imposed a different age limit. (NOTE: An engineless dinghy need not be steered by someone over 16.) Crew must be able to hear orders given from the wheelhouse and the helmsman must be able to hear replies. The helmsman must have a good all round view and be able to hear sound signals. If necessary, a mirror should be fitted to ensure all round visibility and, in certain circumstances, a look out or listening post should be set up.

You must have on board the boat's certificate of registry and navigation regulations for the waterway, unless the authorities concerned have waived this requirement.

The boat's name or number should be indelibly written on the outside of the hull, in Latin characters, at least 10 centimetres high – either in dark letters on a light background, or vice versa. If the registration number is not shown, the owner's name and address must be displayed in a conspicuous place. Your tender should also be identified.

PROTECTION OF THE WATERWAY AND ITS USERS

Do not do anything which could damage waterway installations. Do not attach lines to signs, buoys etc. Do not let potentially damaging objects protrude from your boat. If you damage or displace any installation, or see this has happened, inform the authorities immediately.

Do not put anything into the water which will obstruct or endanger waterway users. Do not put petroleum products into the water. If by accident an object falls in, or a petroleum product is spilled, inform the authorities immediately with details of where the incident occurred. If possible mark the place.

If someone on your boat is in danger, use every possible means to save them. If people on another boat are in danger, or another boat has an accident which might block a channel, give assistance without risking your own safety.

SINKING AND OTHER DIFFICULTIES

If your boat starts to sink, or becomes impossible to control, try to get it clear of the channel. If it sinks, or goes aground, inform the authorities as soon as possible. Someone must stay on, or near, the boat until authorised to leave. If other vessels might run into yours, send people to warn them. The warning should be given sufficiently far from the accident to permit avoiding action. Display signs, or lights, to indicate the side with safe passage (see page 11). If these signs or lights cannot be displayed on the boat they should be placed nearby.

DISTRESS SIGNALS

Visual signals

 A red light, flag or other suitable red object, waved in a circle.

 Repeated slow up and down arm movements.

Red parachute flare or rocket, throwing out red stars.  Flames and smoke from burning oily waste. Red flag with ball, or object like a ball.

Sound signals

The repetition of a long horn blast ▬ ▬ ▬ ...., a bell peal, a whistle blast or the Morse Code SOS:
▬ ▬ ▬ ▬ ▬ ▬ ▬ ▬ ▬

TEMPORARY REQUIREMENTS

In addition to regulations laid down in this Code, boatmasters are required to comply with temporary requirements issued by authorities, in special circumstances, and published as notices.

GENERAL SOUND SIGNALS

The following distress signals and general signals are likely to be made by small craft: Attention ▬ /I am going to my right ▬ /I am going to my left ▬ ▬ /I am going astern ▬ ▬ ▬ /I cannot manoeuvre ▬ ▬ ▬ ▬ / Imminent danger of collision •••••• ...... /I need medical help ▬ ▬ ▬ ▬

 Vessels may be required to make a sound signal when this sign is displayed. The required signal may be shown on an additional panel, eg 'Please open the bridge/lock'.

DEFINITIONS USED IN THIS CODE

Small craft:

When the phrase 'small craft' is used in CEVNI it doesn't necessarily mean a little boat. In official inland waterway terms, any vessel that is under 20 metres in hull length (except ferries, passenger boats carrying more than 12 people and vessels such as pushers, which are designed to propel other vessels) are referred to as 'small craft'. (NOTE: On certain waterways, authorities may use 15 metres as the dividing length between small craft and normal vessels.)

Vessel: Sea-going and inland waterway craft (including small craft & ferries) and floating equipment.

Motorised vessel: Any of the above with mechanical means of propulsion.

Sailing vessel: Vessel using sails as its only means of propulsion. Vessels which are 'motor sailing' are classed as motorised vessels.

Floating equipment: Floating machinery for work on waterways, ports; examples are cranes and dredging equipment on a special platform.

Floating establishment:

Any fixed floating structure, such as a boathouse, pontoon etc is referred to as a 'floating establishment'.

Ferry: Vessel providing transport across a waterway.

Pushed barge: Vessel designed or equipped to be pushed.

Pusher: Motorised vessel designed to push non-motorised barge.

Shipborne barge: Inland waterway vessel that goes to sea on board another vessel.

Assembly of floating material: Navigable rafts etc that do not fit previous descriptions.

Convoy:

'Convoy' has a specific meaning in inland waterway terms. It is a joined group of vessels, floating establishments or assemblies of floating material.

Towed convoy: Group of vessels pulled by one or more motorised vessels.

Pushed convoy: Rigid group of vessels, pushed from behind by a motorised vessel.

Side-by-side formation: Group of vessels, navigating side-by-side, with one group providing motive power.

Stationary vessel: Vessel anchored, attached to the shore or grounded.

Vessel under way: Opposite of stationary vessel.

Vessel engaged in fishing: One using nets, lines, trawls or other gear which restricts manoeuvrability.

Night: Sunset to sunrise.

Day: Sunrise to sunset.

LIGHTS & SYMBOLS ON VESSELS

Light definitions used in this text

Masthead light: Strong white light, projecting an uninterrupted beam throughout a horizontal arc of 225° and placed so as to project this beam from the bow to 22°30' abaft the beam on each side.

Side lights: Bright green light to starboard and bright red light to port, each projecting an uninterrupted beam throughout a horizontal arc of 112°30' and placed so as to project this beam from the bow to 22°30' abaft the beam on each side.

Stern light: Ordinary or bright white light, projecting an uninterrupted beam throughout a horizontal arc of 135° and placed so as to project this beam throughout an arc of 67°30' to each side of the stern.

Light visible all round: Light projecting an uninterrupted beam throughout a horizontal arc of 360°.

MARKINGS ON VESSELS UNDER WAY

Towed convoys

Vessels being towed or temporarily led by an auxiliary display a yellow ball, visible all round.

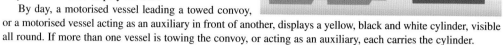

If there are more than two towed vessels side-by-side, only the outer ones display the ball.

By day, a motorised vessel leading a towed convoy, or a motorised vessel acting as an auxiliary in front of another, displays a yellow, black and white cylinder, visible all round. If more than one vessel is towing the convoy, or acting as an auxiliary, each carries the cylinder.

NOTE: Small craft which are towing only another small craft and small craft under tow DO NOT display the above lights or symbols.

By night, a single motorised vessel, temporarily preceded by an auxiliary vessel, only displays the normal markings for a single vessel underway.

By night, a single motorised vessel towing a convoy, or another motorised vessel, displays two masthead lights. A yellow stern light is displayed where it can be seen by towed vessels.

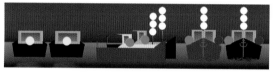

By night, when more than one motorised vessel is towing a convoy or another motorised vessel, each vessel displays three masthead lights. A yellow stern light is displayed by each vessel, where it can be seen by towed vessels.

By night, each towed vessel in a convoy usually carries at least one white light visible all round. A vessel over 110 metres long carries two such lights – one forward and one aft – but convoys are exempted from carrying a total of more than four such lights, providing the outline of the convoy can be clearly seen. The rearmost vessels display white stern lights.

When the vessels in a towed convoy are seagoing vessels, coming from or leaving the sea, they are not required to carry the white lights shown above. Instead, they may display their red and green side lights. If at the rear they also show their stern light.

Single motorised vessels, other than ferries & small craft

By day, normal motorised vessels under way do not display any special signals, except when carrying a dangerous cargo.

At night, they carry a white masthead light, side lights, which are behind and below the masthead light, and a white stern light.

They may carry a second masthead light towards the stern – higher than the forward light. This second light is compulsory on vessels over 110 metres long.

NOTE: When vessels are passing under bridges and cables, or through certain locks, lights may be lowered.

Pushed convoys

NOTE: For the application of lighting regulations, a pushed convoy not greater than 110 metres by 12 metres, is regarded as a single motorised vessel.

By day, pushed convoys under way do not display any special signals, except when carrying a dangerous cargo.

By night, a pushed convoy, consisting of a pusher and single barge, displays a triangle of three masthead lights on the leading vessel. The pusher has three white stern lights and side lights are displayed at the widest point, as near as possible to the pusher.

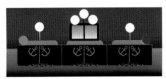

If there are vessels to each side of the pusher, side lights are shown at the widest part of the convoy and vessels to the side show only a masthead light, below the triangle of lights.

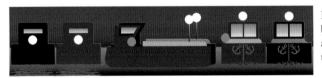

If there is only one vessel to the side of the pusher, the triangle of lights may be carried by the pusher or the pushed vessel, whichever is to port.

Side-by-side formations

By day, side-by-side formations under way display no special signals, except when carrying a dangerous cargo.

By night, each motorised vessel in a side-by-side formation carries a masthead light and stern light. Side lights are shown by the outer vessels.

Instead of a masthead light, non-motorised vessels may show a white light, visible all round, placed no higher than the masthead lights of other vessels.

Sailing vessels

By day, small sailing vessels do not display any signals unless they are using their engine. Then, they display a black cone, point down, placed where it can be easily seen.

NOTE: On certain isolated waterways the requirement to display the cone may be waived.

By day, normal sailing vessels show no special symbols unless they are motor sailing, except that some countries require certain charter vessels to fly a masthead pennant.

By night, normal sailing vessels show side and stern lights. They may, in addition, carry red over green lights, visible all round, at or near the top of the mast.

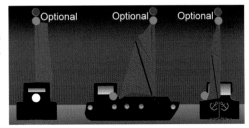

Small sailing craft

By day, small sailing craft show no special symbols, unless they are motor sailing.

By night, small sailing craft show either of the following configurations of bright or ordinary lights: side lights in a single bow light, plus a stern light;

side and stern lights incorporated in a single light carried at the masthead.

A small sailing craft, which is under 7 metres long, may carry a single white masthead light, visible all round, providing it shows a second white light at the approach of other vessels.

Motorised small craft

By day, motorised small craft display no special signs. By night they show either of the following configuration of bright or ordinary lights:

bright or ordinary side lights and a bright light, visible all round, at the masthead;

or bright or ordinary side lights, incorporated in a single bow light, and a bright light, visible all round, at the masthead.

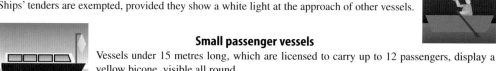

Small craft in tows or side-by-side formations

By night, when a small craft is towing only other small craft or propelling them in side-by-side formation, it shows lights as above.

Other small craft

When proceeding alone by night, small craft which are neither motorised nor under sail carry a white light visible all round.

Ships' tenders are exempted, provided they show a white light at the approach of other vessels.

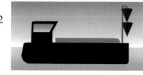

Small passenger vessels

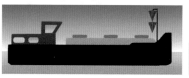

Vessels under 15 metres long, which are licensed to carry up to 12 passengers, display a yellow bicone, visible all round.

NOTE: On some navigations passenger vessels up to 20 metres long may be required to display this bicone.

Vessels carrying dangerous cargoes

By day, vessels carrying dangerous cargo display blue cones. There may be 1, 2 or 3 cones depending on the nature of the dangerous cargo.

NOTE: In France, vessels carrying dangerous cargo may display red cones, instead of blue ones.

Vessels carrying dangerous cargoes (continued)

By night, the corresponding number of blue lights is displayed. The cones or lights are visible all round.

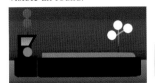

NOTE: Vessels which carry red cones, by day, in France, display red lights instead of blue ones, by night.

When a dangerous cargo is carried by a pushed convoy, the blue lights or cones are displayed on the pusher.

When a dangerous cargo is carried by a side-to-side formation, the propelling vessel carries the cones and lights.

NOTE: Seagoing vessels, temporarily operating on inland waters and carrying dangerous goods, may be authorised to display the dangerous cargo symbol from the International Code of Signals instead of blue cones.

Ferries

By day, ferries display a green ball, visible all round, unless the authorities have waived this requirement.

By day, ferries which are moving under their own power and have priority display a white cylinder under the ball.

By night, ferries which are not moving independently display only a green light over a white light, both visible all round.

By night, ferries which are moving under their own power show green over white lights, visible all round, together with side and stern lights.

By night, ferries which are moving under their own power and have priority display a second green light, visible all round, over green and white lights.

By night, the lead boat, or float, of a pendulum ferry carries a white light, visible all round.

NOTE: The authorities may require passenger boats which are operating a regular service on isolated waterways or lakes to carry the lights displayed by ferries.

Signs giving advance warnings of ferries

 Ferry moving independently, 1500 metres ahead.

 Ferry not moving independently.

 Attention! Bac (= Ferry) ahead.

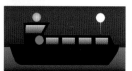

Additional markings for official vessels

Certain vessels which are carrying out work whilst under way (eg survey ships) show a yellow scintillating light.

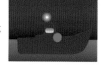

Vessels of the waterway authorities and fire service/police boats show a blue scintillating light when on official duties.

These lights are in addition to any other symbols/lights the vessel usually carries.

Additional markings for pilot boats

By day, pilot vessels display a flag which, depending on the country, may be blue or red and bear the letter L or P.

By night, pilot boats display a white light over a red light, both visible all round, in place of the normal masthead light. Normal side and stern lights are shown.

Vessels having priority of passage

Vessels which have priority of passage, at points where the order of passage is regulated, display a long red pennant at the bow.

Floating establishments

By night, floating establishments and assemblies of floating materials display enough lights, visible all round, to illuminate their outline.

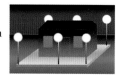

Vessels whose ability to manoeuvre is limited

By day, a vessel carrying out work which limits its capacity to give way, in accordance with these regulations, shows a black bicone between two black balls, visible all round.

By night, the symbols are replaced by a white light between two red lights. These lights are shown in addition to others which the vessel is normally required to carry.

By day, if the vessels described above are causing an obstruction, in addition to the symbols described, they display black balls where the passage is obstructed and black bicones where the passage is possible. The symbols are visible all round.

By night, the symbols are replaced by red lights where the passage is obstructed and green lights where the passage is possible.

NOTE: All vessels must give way to vessels whose ability to manoeuvre is limited.

Fishing vessels

Trolling with vessels abreast is prohibited, other than in areas where the authorities have waived this provision. All vessels should keep well clear of the stern of a vessel which is trawling or dragging other fishing equipment. All vessels, other than those whose manoeuvrability is limited, must give way to vessels engaged in fishing.

By day, vessels which are trawling, or dragging other fishing equipment, display two black cones, visible all round.

By night, the cones are replaced by a green light over a white light. These are in addition to lights normally displayed and are shown below the masthead light (if fitted) and above side lights.

NOTE: Fishing vessels under 50 metres long are not required to display a masthead light.

By day, vessels that are engaged in another form of fishing display two black cones, visible all round.

By night, the cones are replaced by a red light over a white light and the normal masthead light (if fitted) is extinguished.

NOTE: The single black cone, or white light, shown in the above illustrations is only displayed if fishing gear extends more than 150 metres to the side of the vessel.

By day, nets or poles which extend into or near the channel are marked by yellow floats or yellow flags.

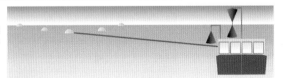

By night, the nets or poles are marked by white lights, visible all round.

NOTE: Vessels under 20 metres, which are engaged in any form of fishing, may display a basket instead of 2 black cones.

Vessel engaged in mine sweeping

By day, vessels engaged in mine sweeping display a triangle of black balls, visible all round.

By night, the balls are replaced with green lights, visible all round. These lights are additional to any which would normally be used.

NOTE: Other vessels must keep at least 1000 metres from the rear of a vessel engaged in mine sweeping.

Vessels used for diving

Vessels used for diving display one or more rigid blue/white panels – a reproduction of the 'A' flag of the International Code of Signals.

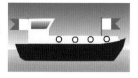

Diving for pleasure must not be practised on the route of a ferry, near harbour entrances, near berthing areas, in areas reserved for water skiing or similar activities and in situations where navigation might be hindered.

WATER SKIING AND SIMILAR ACTIVITIES

Water skiing and similar activities are only permitted in daylight and good visibility. The operator of a vessel towing a water skier must be accompanied by a competent person, responsible for the tow and skier.

If the skier loses grip of the tow rope, the person responsible for the skier must haul it into the towing vessel, as fast as possible. Except when in a channel reserved for their exclusive use, towing vessels, skiers, personal watercraft etc must keep clear of other vessels. Many authorities only permit these activities to take place in designated areas.

Signs indicating a designated area for certain activities

Area designated for:

Pleasure craft	Water skiing	Sailing boats	Manually operated craft
Sail boards	High speed craft	Launching	Motorised craft	Personal watercraft

Signs prohibiting certain activities

Forbidden in area with sign displayed:

Pleasure craft	Water skiing	Sailing boats	Manually operated craft
Sail boards	High speed craft	Launching	Motorised craft	Personal watercraft

This sign indicates an area not intended for navigation. Access is prohibited, except for non-motorised small craft.

8 This sign indicates that a speed limit is in force. It is forbidden to exceed 8 kph.

Buoys marking restricted areas

Areas where usage is restricted or prohibited are marked by yellow buoys. As far as possible the nature of restriction is made clear on charts, or by additional marks on buoys or on the bank. Here, a topmark in the shape of a rigid red pennant, together with general prohibitory signs on the bank, indicates that navigation is totally prohibited.

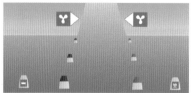

Yellow buoys and advisory signs are also used to mark channels which can be used by vessels etc in areas where they would otherwise be prohibited. Here, signs on banks indicate that motorised vessels may pass through the channel; signs on buoys indicate that one area is designated for sailboards and another for manually propelled craft.

VESSELS UNABLE TO MANOEUVRE

By day, vessels which are unable to manoeuvre display two black balls, visible all round, one above the other. Alternatively, someone on board waves a red flag in a half circle.

By night, vessels which are unable to manoeuvre display two red lights visible all round, one above the other. These lights are shown in addition to other lights which the vessel would normally be required to carry. Alternatively, someone on board waves a red flag in a half circle.

By night, someone on board a small craft unable to manoeuvre may swing a white light, instead of a red one.

If necessary a vessel will make the sound signal ▬ ▬ ▬ ▬ 'I am unable to manoeuvre.'

COURSE TO PASS VESSELS, FLOATING EQUIPMENT ETC; AT WORK, GROUNDED OR SUNK

By day, the side on which the channel is clear is marked by two green bicones, or the green and white general permission sign, visible all round; the side on which the channel is not clear is marked by a red ball, or the red and white general prohibitory sign, visible all round.

Channel is clear on both sides.

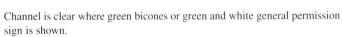

Channel is clear where green bicones or green and white general permission sign is shown.

By night, green or red lights replace the above symbols/signs.

If the vessel or equipment needs protection from wash: by day, the clear side of the channel is marked by a red flag or board over a white flag or board, visible all round.

Channel is clear on both sides, but vessel needs protection from wash.

Channel is clear when red over white is displayed, but vessel needs protection from wash.

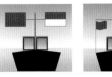

By night, white or red lights replace the above symbols/signs.

11

STATIONARY VESSELS

Vessels made fast to the bank, excluding ferries & floating establishments

By day, a vessel made fast to the bank displays no symbols, unless required to by other regulations.

By night, a vessel made fast to the bank shows a white light, visible all round, on the side nearest to the channel.

NOTE: Authorities may exempt vessels, especially small craft, from the need to show this light when it is obviously not necessary, eg if the vessel is clearly lit from the bank.

Anchored vessels, excluding vessels which are aground, sunk or working

By day, an anchored vessel carries a black ball, visible all round.

NOTE: This is not mandatory when the waterway is temporarily closed to navigation or when the vessel is in a safe situation outside the channel. Waterways authorities may make other exemptions.

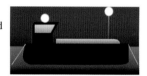

By night, a single vessel stationary offshore carries two white lights, one forward and one aft, visible all round. The forward light is higher.

NOTE: A small craft which is stationary offshore may display one white light, visible all round, instead of two.

Pushed convoys

By night, when a pushed convoy is stationary offshore, the white lights, visible all round, are displayed on all vessels in the convoy and a lower light is displayed on the pusher.

If the pusher leaves the convoy, the rearmost vessel displays the lower light.

NOTE: If there are more than four vessels in the convoy, it need not carry more than four lights, providing the outline can clearly be seen on the channel side.

Ferries

By night, when a ferry is made fast to its landing stage, it carries the symbols or lights which it displays when moving.

Except that a ferry which has priority extinguishes the upper green light as soon as it goes out of service.

Floating establishments

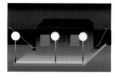

By night, floating establishments, or assemblies of floating materials, must, when berthed, display a sufficient number of white lights, visible all round, to enable their outline to be clearly seen on the channel side.

STATIONARY VESSELS (CONTINUED)

Vessels whose anchors may be a danger to navigation

By day, an anchor which may be a danger to navigation is marked by a yellow float and a radar reflector.

By night, the anchor is marked by a float, a radar reflector and a white light, visible all round. The 'stationary vessel' light, which is nearest to the anchor, is replaced by two white lights.

Vessels carrying dangerous cargo

In addition to the above markings, stationary vessels carrying dangerous cargo display the blue cones or lights which they display when underway.

MEETING, CROSSING & OVERTAKING

Definitions used in this text

Give way vessel: The vessel which, when two vessels are meeting or crossing, has to give way to the other.
Stand on vessel: The vessel which, when two vessels are meeting or crossing, maintains its course and speed.
Upstream vessel: A vessel proceeding towards the source of a river or ascending locks.
Downstream vessel: A vessel proceeding away from the source of a river or descending locks.
Right bank: The bank which is on the right of a vessel which is proceeding downstream.
Left bank: The bank which is on the left of a vessel which is proceeding downstream.

NOTE: On summit levels and broad expanses of water, upstream and downstream may be defined by authorities.

General principles

Crossing or overtaking is only permitted when the channel is unquestionably wide enough for simultaneous passage, taking into account local circumstances and vessel movement.

Vessels on a course which precludes danger of collision must not change their course and speed in a manner which gives rise to danger of collision.

A stand on vessel which finds itself close to and in danger of collision with a give way vessel must manoeuvre to avoid collision, if the collision could not be avoided solely by a manoeuvre by the give way vessel.

Hydrofoils and hovercraft are required to leave all other vessels room to hold course and to manoeuvre.

Obligations of small craft

Apart from certain specific rules that state otherwise, small craft must always give way to normal vessels, other than hydrofoils and hovercraft.

It is incumbent on small craft to leave other vessels (except hydrofoils and hovercraft) sufficient room to hold their course and to manoeuvre.

Waterway classification

Rivers are generally Class 1 waterways. Canals, lakes and broad waterways are generally Class 2, but authorities may classify individual waterways differently.

Crossing rules

When two normal vessels are crossing in such a manner that there is risk of collision, the vessel that has the other vessel to starboard gives way and, if possible, avoids crossing ahead of it.

When two motorised small craft are crossing in such a manner that there is risk of collision, the vessel that has the other vessel to starboard gives way and, if possible, avoids crossing ahead of it.

When a normal vessel crosses the path of a small craft, which is to its starboard, it maintains course and speed.

Motorised small craft give way to non-motorised small craft. Small craft, which are neither motoring nor under sail, give way to small craft under sail.

Crossing rules (continued)

When two small sailing craft are on a potential collision course, and on a different tack, the one with the wind to port gives way.

When two sailing craft are on a potential collision course, and on the same tack, the vessel upwind gives way.

When a sailing craft, with the wind on its port side, sees another sailing craft on a potential collision course to windward, it gives way if it cannot determine which tack the other craft is on.

When a small sailing craft is overtaking another, the overtaking craft should pass on the side on which the overtaken craft has the wind.

When another category of small craft is being overtaken by a small sailing craft, it should, if necessary and safe to do so, manoeuvre to allow the overtaking to take place on the side in which the overtaking craft has the wind.

A normal vessel which is following the starboard side of a marked channel maintains its speed and course even when it is in sight of another normal vessel to which it would generally give way. Similarly, a small craft which is following the starboard side of a marked channel maintains its speed and course when it is in sight of another small craft to which it would generally give way.

Normal meeting rules – *Class 1 waterways*

Taking into account local situations and vessel movements, normal vessels which are travelling downstream have priority over those travelling upstream but upstream vessels choose which side they will give way on.

Upstream vessels, which are leaving a course for downstream vessels on their port side, make no signal.

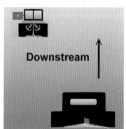

By day, upstream vessels, which are leaving a course for downstream vessels to starboard, display a waved blue flag, a bright scintillating white light, or a light blue board (with or without a bright scintillating light at its centre) to starboard.

By night, the board with scintillating light, or light alone, is used.

NOTE: For clarity, from here on, the text will only refer to a blue board.

Downstream vessels acknowledge that they understand that the upstream vessels are leaving a course to starboard by also displaying a blue board on their starboard side.

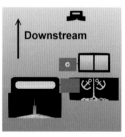

These signals can be seen, whether the boat concerned is ahead or astern, and are displayed until passing is complete. They must not be displayed after passing, except when upstream vessels intend to go on leaving a starboard passing course for downstream vessels.

If upstream vessels believe that downstream vessels have not understood their intentions, about the side they are leaving a course on, they make a sound signal.

Normal meeting rules – *Class 1 waterways* (continued)

We will pass port to port.

We will pass starboard to starboard.

Downstream vessels acknowledge the course left for them by the upstream vessels by sounding: 1 short blast when meeting port to port; 2 short blasts when meeting is to be starboard to starboard.

Departures from normal meeting rules – *Class 1 waterways*

Providing that they are certain that their request can be safely carried out, certain categories of downstream vessels may request upstream vessels to change the course they have left for them. These are: passenger vessels on regular service, carrying a specific minimum number of passengers, that wish to call at a landing stage on the side used by upstream vessels; towed convoys that are coming downstream but intend to turn upstream.

If such downstream vessels wish to pass port to port they sound one short blast, if they wish to pass starboard to starboard they sound two short blasts and display a blue board on their starboard side.

Upstream vessels then manoeuvre, as necessary, to permit the requested passing. If the passing is to be port to port, upstream vessels sound one short blast. If the passing is to be starboard to starboard, upstream vessels sound two short blasts and display a blue board at their starboard side.

None of the above applies to meetings between small craft and normal vessels, nor to meetings between small craft, nor meetings between sailing vessels. These categories give way as indicated in the section on **General Principles for Meeting, Crossing & Overtaking**.

When an upstream vessel sees that the course requested by a downstream vessel could lead to a collision, it sounds a series of very short blasts. •••••• Both vessels must then take avoiding action to prevent collision.

Normal meeting rules – *Class 2 waterways*

When two normal vessels are coming towards each other and there appears to be a risk of collision, each alters course to starboard to pass port to port. When a normal vessel is coming towards a small craft and there appears to be a risk of collision, the small craft shall alter its course as necessary to allow the normal vessel room to pass safely.

Small craft meeting

When two motorised small craft are coming towards each other and there appears to be a risk of collision, each alters course to starboard to pass port to port. When two small craft of different categories are coming towards each other and there appears to be a risk of collision, the rules for different categories of small craft crossing shall apply.

Departure from normal meeting rules – *Class 2 waterways*

Provided they are certain that their request can be safely carried out, normal vessels may, in certain circumstances, request to pass starboard to starboard. Examples are: vessels needing to stop at a bank, or enter a harbour on their left; light vessels which cannot keep to the right because of a side wind. In such cases, vessels sound two short blasts and display a blue board on their starboard side. The vessel being met then manoeuvres to leave sufficient space to starboard and, at the same time, sounds two short blasts and displays a blue board to starboard.

If the vessel being met sees that the course requested could lead to a collision, it sounds a series of very short blasts. •••••• Both vessels must then take avoiding action to prevent collision.

MEETING, CROSSING & OVERTAKING (CONTINUED)

Meetings in narrow channels

Advance warning of a narrow channel may be given by positioning this sign on the bank. Numbers indicate the width of the channel in metres.

A narrow channel should be navigated as quickly as is prudently possible. If the view is restricted, 1 long blast should be sounded before entering. It should be periodically repeated if the section is long.

Small craft must give way to normal vessels that are approaching or passing through a narrow channel.

When two small craft are approaching, or are in a narrow channel, the rules which apply between themselves are the same as those which apply between normal vessels.

Narrow channels on waterways where 'upstream' and 'downstream' are defined

An upstream vessel, which can see that a downstream vessel (other than a small craft) is approaching a narrow channel, should wait below the channel until the other has passed. A downstream vessel, which can see that an upstream vessel has entered the channel, should wait above the channel until it has passed.

Narrow channels on waterways where 'upstream' and 'downstream' are not defined

Vessels with no obstacle to starboard and those with the outside of a curved channel to starboard hold their course (except for small craft). Other vessels wait until they have passed.

If a small craft under sail and a small craft of another category are likely to meet in a narrow channel, sailing boats proceed and other craft await their passing. Except that, when a sailing craft is to leeward, the other craft maintains its course and the sailing boat waits until it has passed.

If two normal sailing boats, or two sailing boats which are small craft, are likely to meet in a narrow channel, windward craft have priority. If both are going with the wind, craft with wind to starboard have priority.

When a normal sailing boat and a sailing boat that is a small craft are likely to meet, the normal sailing craft has priority.

If vessels meet in a narrow channel they must do everything possible to pass at a point and under conditions that involve the minimum danger. If collision is likely, a series of very short blasts •••• should be given.

Meetings prohibited by signs

This sign prohibits meeting and overtaking. When it is displayed on waterways where 'upstream' and 'downstream' are defined, a vessel proceeding upstream, which can see that a downstream vessel is approaching, should wait until the other vessel has passed.

On waterways where 'upstream' and 'downstream' are not defined the rules previously given for meeting in narrow channels apply.

When an alternate one way system is used to prevent meetings in certain sections, passage is prohibited when any of the general prohibitory signs is displayed and permitted when any of the general permission signs is displayed.

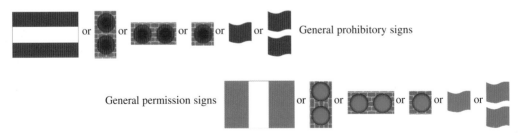

MEETING, CROSSING & OVERTAKING (CONTINUED)

Signs warning of meetings – Rhine traffic signals

In certain parts of the river Rhine, luminous white bars advise upstream vessels about the presence and type of downstream traffic in the sector ahead:

 No vessel

 At least one single vessel

 At least one convoy, under 110m

 At least one convoy, over 110m

Advance warning signs

Depending on the local circumstances, advance warning of signs prohibiting or permitting passage may be given by one of these signs.

Keep an especially sharp lookout

Stop as required by regulations

White lights mean that there is a difficulty ahead:

Fixed means stop as required by regulations.

Isophase means proceed. or

Overtaking definitions used in this text

Overtaking vessel: Vessel overtaking, or intending to overtake, another.
Overtaken vessel: Vessel being overtaken, or about to be overtaken.

Basic overtaking rules

The overtaking vessel must make certain that the manoeuvre can be accomplished without danger.

Except when being overtaken by a small craft, the overtaken vessel will, if necessary, slow down and take any other necessary steps to enable the manoeuvre to be carried out quickly and safely.

Normally, the overtaking vessel passes down the port side of the overtaken vessel but, if the channel is sufficiently wide, it may pass down the starboard side.

A small sailing craft should overtake another small sailing craft on the side where the overtaken craft has the wind.

When a small sailing craft is overtaking another type of small craft, the overtaken craft shall, if possible, manoeuvre to allow the overtaking to take place on the side where the sailing craft has the wind.

Sound signals made by vessels during overtaking

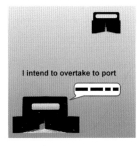

Sound signals are given by the overtaking vessel when overtaking is impossible without the overtaken vessel changing course, or when the overtaken vessel appears to be unaware that the manoeuvre will take place.

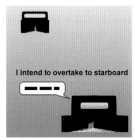

17

Sound signals made by vessels during overtaking (continued)

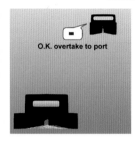

If the vessel being overtaken agrees that it is possible for the overtaking vessel to pass on the indicated side, it makes the appropriate sound signal and moves over if necessary.

If the vessel being overtaken sees that it is not possible for the overtaking to take place on the indicated side, but is possible on the other side, it makes the appropriate sound signal.

If the overtaking vessel then wishes to pass on the side indicated by the overtaken vessel it makes the appropriate signal. The overtaken vessel then leaves the required space, moving over if necessary.

In all cases, if the overtaken vessel does not believe the overtaking can be safely carried out, it sounds 5 short blasts. ▬ ▬ ▬ ▬ ▬

NOTE: Small craft do not usually make sound signals when overtaking normal vessels or other small craft however a boatmaster who believes that an overtaking manoeuvre could lead to danger should make the appropriate sound signal.

Overtaking prohibited by signs

No overtaking

No overtaking of convoys by convoys *

No meeting or overtaking

* This does not apply if at least one vessel is a pushed convoy not larger than 110 metres x 12 metres

NAVIGATING IN THE PROXIMITY OF OTHER VESSELS

Do not enter the spaces between vessels in a towed convoy.

Do not sail abreast unless this can be done without inconvenience or danger to shipping.

Do not come alongside another vessel, to grapple it, or ride in its wake, without the boatmaster's permission.

Keep at least 50 metres from vessels displaying two or three blue cones or lights, except when passing or overtaking.

DO NOT APPROACH

Any vessel carrying dangerous materials, on which accident or incident has provoked a release of dangerous materials which the crew cannot control, gives a 'DO NOT APPROACH' signal. This is the repetition, for 15 consecutive minutes, of one short blast followed by one long blast, accompanied by a synchronised light signal.

Anyone hearing that signal must take every precaution to avoid danger, which, above all, means putting as much distance as possible between their vessel and the vessel concerned. Other precautions include closing hatches, portholes etc, stopping smoking, extinguishing naked flames, ceasing any action which may create sparks and closing down any auxiliary motors which are not needed.

Vessels motoring through the danger zone may need to turn round and go back but, when considering that option, the effect of current must be taken into account.

Those aboard vessels which are moored in the danger zone should take the above precautions and then abandon ship.

CROSSING A WATERWAY, ENTERING/LEAVING A TRIBUTARY OR HARBOUR

General principles

Vessels should only cross the waterway, or enter/leave a tributary or harbour, if they can do so safely and without obliging other vessels to make abrupt change in speed or course. Downstream normal vessels, which have to turn upstream in order to enter a tributary/harbour, must give way to upstream vessels that also wish to enter the tributary/harbour, unless the upstream vessels are small craft. Downstream small craft must give way to upstream small craft.

Signs and lights on major waterways and tributaries

When yellow lights flash on the bank, boats on the main waterway must, if necessary, alter course or speed to allow vessels to leave harbours or tributaries.

When one of these signs is displayed, vessels may only cross the waterway, or enter/leave a tributary or harbour, if they can do so without obliging vessels on the major waterway to modify their speed or course.

The following tributary signs are advisory:

You are on the major waterway

Major waterway ahead

NOTE: Other variations on these signs may be displayed.

Sound signals

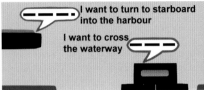

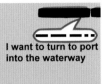

When entering and leaving tributaries/harbours, vessels (other than small craft) must give a sound signal if their manoeuvre might oblige other vessels to alter course or speed.

If necessary, vessels crossing the channel make an additional signal before completing the crossing.

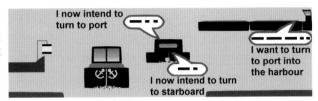

Vessels which hear these signals make any necessary alterations in course and speed.

Signs prohibiting or permitting leaving or entering tributaries and harbours

When this combination of signs is on a main waterway, vessels may not enter a tributary or harbour (in the direction of the arrow). When it is near the exit of a tributary or harbour, vessels may not leave.

When this sign is on a main waterway, vessels may enter a tributary or harbour. When it is near the exit of a tributary or harbour, vessels may leave.

TRAILING ANCHORS

Trailing anchors, cables and chains is forbidden, except for small movements at stopping places. Even those small movements are forbidden when this sign is displayed.

When this sign is displayed on the bank, anchoring is permitted on the side where the sign is placed.

DRIFTING

Drifting is forbidden, except for small movements at stopping places. However, vessels which are being pushed downstream are not considered to be 'drifting' if they are facing upstream and have their engines running.

WASH

Vessels must not create wash or suction which could damage vessels and structures. In particular, they must slow down – but not to below safe steering speed – outside harbour entrances, near stationary vessels and ferry boats which are not moving independently and when this 'Do not make wash' sign is displayed.

When passing a vessel which is displaying red over white flags, boards or lights to indicate that it must be protected from wash, vessels must reduce speed and keep as far off as possible.

SECTIONS WHERE THE COURSE IS PRESCRIBED

In sections where the course to be followed is prescribed by signs shown below, upstream normal vessels must not impede downstream normal vessels and upstream small craft must not impede downstream small craft. In particular, when approaching either of the signs which require crossing of the channel, upstream vessels must slow down, or even stop, to allow downstream vessels to manoeuvre.

 Go in direction of arrow

 Move to left of channel

 Move to right of channel

 Keep to left of channel

 Keep to right of channel

 Cross channel to port

 Cross channel to starboard

Additional signs may give the reason for the prescribed course. For example:

 Channel is 10 metres from bank

 Section of reduced depth

The end of the need to follow the prescribed course may be indicated by this 'End of restriction' sign.

TURNING

Vessels should only turn if they can do so safely and without obliging other vessels to make an abrupt change in speed or course. A normal vessel wishing to make a turning manoeuvre, which will mean that other vessels will have to make any course or speed alteration, must announce its intention, in good time, by a sound signal.

I wish to turn to port ━ ━ ━   I wish to turn to starboard ━ ━

On hearing a signal, other vessels must (as far as it is necessary and possible) make any alterations in course and speed, to enable the turn to be made safely. In particular, if a vessel (other than a small craft) needs to turn into the current, others must manoeuvre in a manner which will facilitate the turn.

Signs prohibiting or permitting turning

Vessels must not turn when this sign is displayed.

This sign indicates a recommended turning area.

LEAVING A BERTH

Vessels should only leave a berth if they can do so safely and without obliging others to make an abrupt change to speed or course. Normal vessels (except ferry boats) wishing to leave a berth without turning, must give a sound signal in good time if the manoeuvre might require other normal vessels to alter course or speed. On hearing a signal, other vessels must, if it is necessary and possible, alter course and speed, to enable the unberthing to be made safely. The signals given are:
━ When the vessels are approaching on the starboard side. ━ ━ When vessels are approaching on the port side.

SUSPENSION OF NAVIGATION

When it is necessary to suspend navigation on a waterway and one of the general signs is shown, vessels must stop before the sign.

Rhine flood warnings

  Flood level indicators 1 & 2 are installed at various points. All navigation ceases when water reaches flood level 2. Navigation restrictions are in force when level is between 1 & 2; these are given in RPNR.

PASSAGE THROUGH FIXED BRIDGES

Markings on bridge spans

 Passage is prohibited outside the area between white triangles.

 Passage through the area between green triangles is recommended.

Passage through span is forbidden. Or or or

 Recommended route for all traffic. Span open to traffic in both directions.

Recommended route for traffic travelling in this direction. Span closed to traffic coming the other way. 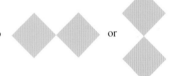 or

NOTE: When some bridge spans are marked by one or more yellow diamonds, vessels using unmarked spans do so at their own risk.

PASSAGE THROUGH TUNNELS, MOVABLE BRIDGES & LOCKS

General principles

Vessels equipped with radio should listen on the installation's channel. Boatmasters must obey instructions given by waterway staff to ensure safe, orderly navigation and quick passage, even if those instructions contradict this Code. Vessels must not overtake on approaches to bridges, tunnels and locks unless instructed to do so by waterway staff. Vessels should approach, pass through or enter at reduced speed.

A vessel not wishing to pass through a tunnel or bridge, or enter a lock, must stop before this sign which means 'Stop as required by regulations'.

Vessels must not enter or leave a lock, or pass through a tunnel or bridge, when any red light is shown, unless instructed to do so by staff. (That does not apply to vessels of reduced height, using a span showing a yellow light or lights.)

PASSAGE THROUGH TUNNELS, MOVABLE BRIDGES & LOCKS (CONTINUED)

Lights and signs on movable bridges and at tunnel & lock entrances/exits

 Out of service. or or Passage/entry/exit prohibited.

Passage/entry prohibited but installation is being prepared. Be ready to get underway. or or

 or or  or Passage/entry/exit permitted.

Passage by vessels of reduced height permitted, in both directions. or

 or or or Passage by vessels of reduced height permitted, in this direction. Closed to traffic coming the other way.

NOTE: Vessels of reduced height, passing through movable spans which are closed, do so at their own risk.

Sluices

When a red ball, or one of these light configurations, is displayed at a lock it is being used, or is about to be used, as a sluice. Vessels should keep clear. or or or

Signs indicating headroom on bridges

Headroom (metres) can be read from scale on bridge pier.

 Figure shown (metres) is subtracted from that indicated on scale, to give headroom at lowest point of span.

Figure shown (metres) is headroom under span on which sign is placed.

Lock regulations

Vessels equipped with a radio telephone should listen on the lock's channel. When the channel is indicated on this sign, vessels (other than small craft) must establish radio contact with the lock.

 This blue sign gives the lock channel, but does not require vessels to establish radio contact.

NOTE: The above signs may be displayed at installations other than locks. Their meaning is the same in all situations.

Lock regulations (continued)

Except for small craft, the normal rule at locks is 'first come, first served' but the following have priority:
Fire, police or customs vessels of countries bordering the waterways, on urgent duty; vessels to which authorities have expressly granted priority, such as passenger vessels on regular service. Vessels which are entitled to priority display a red pennant at the bow.

Locks must be entered slowly to avoid bumping gates, protective devices, or other vessels.

Where limits are marked on the lock side walls, vessels must keep within them.

Anchors must be fully raised in.

While the lock is being filled or emptied, and until a vessel is permitted to leave, lines should be used to keep the boat close to the wall and to prevent it from bumping parts of the lock or other vessels.

Fenders must be used and, if movable, must be of a floating material.

Water must not be discharged onto lock copings or other vessels.

The use of engines is prohibited, from the time a vessel makes fast until permitted to leave, though some authorities may waive this proviso.

Lock keepers may, in the interest of safe, orderly navigation, issue instructions which contradict these regulations.

Small craft are not entitled to separate locking and must not enter a lock until invited to do so by staff.
When passing through at the same time as other vessels, small craft enter after the latter.
Small craft must keep away from other vessels inside locks.

VESSELS CARRYING DANGEROUS CARGOES

Vessels required to carry 2 or 3 blue cones or lights are never locked with other vessels.
Vessels required to carry 1 blue cone, or light, are never locked with passenger vessels.

WEIRS

Advance warning of a weir may be given by this sign.

Trailing anchors, chains or cable at or near weirs is strictly prohibited.

Passage through an opening in a weir is only permitted when both sides of the opening are marked by one of the general permission signs, such as: or

 Except that, when there is a bridge over the weir, passage is permitted through a span marked with one or more yellow diamonds.

Passage through an opening in a weir is prohibited when the opening is marked by any of the red general prohibitory signs, such as: or

BERTHING

'Berthing' is defined as 'making fast, directly or indirectly, to the bank, or anchoring'.

General berthing rules

Vessels should berth as close to the bank as their draft and local conditions permit and in a manner which does not obstruct shipping. A berthed vessel must be secured in a manner which ensures that it will not change position and thus constitute a possible danger or obstruction to shipping, taking into account possible effects of any wind, tide, water level, suction and wash.

BERTHING (CONTINUED)

General berthing rules (continued)

Vessels may not berth: under bridges; in or near narrow channels in a channel which would become narrow if vessels were berthed there; at entries to, or exits from, tributaries; on the course of ferries; on route to a landing stage; in a designated turning area; under high voltage electric cables, which may be indicated by the symbol on the right.

Signs prohibiting berthing

 No berthing

 No anchoring

 No making fast

No berthing within a width of 30 metres from the sign

No berthing, in the direction of the arrow, for 500 metres

Signs permitting berthing

 Berthing permitted

 Anchoring permitted

 Making fast permitted

 Mooring for pleasure craft, 1500 metres ahead.

Berthing permitted within a width of 50 metres from the sign

Berthing permitted, in the direction of the arrow, for 500 metres

 Berthing abreast permitted, up to the number shown in Roman numerals

 Berthing permitted on the breadth of water which is between 10 and 50 metres from the sign

Roadsteads

On parts of certain other navigations, such as the river Rhine, roadsteads are provided for commercial vessels waiting to load or unload. Roadsteads are marked by this sign and additional markings (as shown on page 26) indicate the type of vessel which may berth there. Other vessels may not stop in the roads unless they have received authorisation from the authorities.

NOTE: This sign means 'There are restrictions on navigation – make enquiries'.

Berthing in the vicinity of vessels carrying a dangerous cargo

Do not berth within 10 metres

Do not berth within 50 metres

Do not berth within 100 metres

Vessels carrying dangerous cargoes may display these signs on board:

No berthing, within the lateral distance shown, in metres, on the sign

 No smoking

 No boarding

BERTHING (CONTINUED)

Berthing reserved for commercial vessels

	Not required to carry any blue cones/lights	Required to carry one blue cone/light	Required to carry 2 blue cones/lights	Required to carry 3 blue cones/lights
For pushing navigation				
For non-pushing navigation				
For all navigation				

All berthing signs apply to the side of the waterway on which a sign is placed.

Watch & surveillance

When a vessel is berthed in the channel a continuous watch must be kept. Vessels outside the channel should, if local conditions indicate that the need for prompt action may occur, or if authorities insist on it, be under the surveillance of someone who is capable of acting quickly if the need arises.

REDUCED VISIBILITY

General principles

Vessels under way, in reduced visibility, must adjust their speed to suit the conditions, circumstances and presence of other vessels.

Unless the waterway authorities have waived this, vessels navigating in reduced visibility must have a radio telephone which can receive and transmit on vessel to vessel and vessel to shore frequencies and be able to keep a listening watch on any channel designated by the authorities.

Vessels must stop if they cannot proceed without danger. In deciding whether it is safe to proceed, vessels using radar must take into account that visibility is reduced for other vessels.

When stopping, vessels must keep as far as possible from the channel.

With certain prescribed exceptions, rules for meeting other vessels do not apply in reduced visibility.

Meeting vessels keep as far as possible to the right and pass port to port.

A vessel navigating by radar may only overtake another vessel when the channel is wide enough and the helmsmen have agreed, by radio, on which side overtaking will take place.

Vessels under way must post a forward look out, who can hear the helmsman. This does not apply to vessels navigating by radar, providing the steersman can hear sound signals.

NOTE: On various navigations, vessels may only navigate by radar if the on board equipment is approved by the authorities and the boatmaster holds a radar diploma for the waterway concerned.

Sound signals when stationary in reduced visibility

Stationary vessels (including grounded vessels) which are in or near the channel and outside a harbour, or designated berthing area, must make a sound signal as soon as they hear a sound signal which indicates that another vessel is approaching.

REDUCED VISIBILITY (CONTINUED)

Sound signals when stationary in reduced visibility (continued)

The stationary vessel will continue to give the signal (at intervals of not more than 1 minute) for as long as the signal of the approaching vessel can be heard. The signals are:

Class 1 waterways

One peal of a bell, for a vessel to the left of the channel (for an observer facing downstream).

Two peals of a bell, for the vessel to the right of the channel.

Three peals of a bell, for the vessel which is uncertain of its position.

Class 2 waterways

One peal of a bell, for a vessel in any position.

Except that some authorities may permit the bell peal to be replaced by one long horn blast, between two short ones.

A vessel not parallel to the side of the channel, or positioned in a way which could endanger other vessels, will sound one of these signals, even if it cannot hear a signal from an approaching vessel.

Collision avoidance when navigating by radar

When a vessel is navigating by radar, in circumstances where navigation would otherwise be impossible, two people who are conversant with radar navigation must be in the wheelhouse.

Vessels navigating by radar which 'see' on their screen vessels, whose position and movements may cause danger, will attempt to contact those vessels by radio telephone. If they do not get a response they must take every possible action to avoid collision.

A vessel navigating by radar must take appropriate action when approaching sections where there may be vessels not yet visible on the screen. In all circumstances, any vessel perceiving a danger must slow down or stop.

NOTE: On the Rhine and certain other navigations, downstream vessels perceiving a danger are expected to take avoiding action by turning upstream, if necessary.

Navigation by radar

Class 1 waterways

Downstream vessels, except small craft, when navigating by radar make a tritonal signal, eg DOH ME SOH. The signal is given when a vessel 'sees', on its screen, vessels which could cause danger or when it is approaching a section where there may be vessels it cannot 'see'. The signal is repeated as often as necessary.

Upstream vessels, navigating alone on radar, on hearing the tritonal signal, make one long blast. ▬

Upstream convoys make two long blasts. ▬▬ These signals are also given when an upstream vessel 'sees', on its screen, vessels which could cause danger or when approaching a section where there may be vessels it cannot 'see'.

Upstream vessels give downstream vessels, by radio, their category, name, position and direction. Small craft state which side they are giving way on, others propose a passing side.

Downstream vessels reply giving their category, name, position and direction. Normal vessels either confirm they will pass on proposed side, or indicate another. Small craft state which side they are giving way on.

Navigation by radar (continued)

Class 2 waterways

▬ Downstream and upstream vessels sound one long blast. The signal is given when a vessel 'sees', on its screen, vessels which could cause danger or when it is approaching a section where there may be vessels it cannot 'see'. The signal is repeated as often as necessary.

▬ ▬ ▬ ▬ ▬ Ferries, on hearing one long blast, sound one long blast followed by four short blasts.

Downstream and upstream vessels use their radio telephone to give oncoming vessels any information necessary for safe navigation. Vessels, including ferries, which are equipped with radio telephones, reply and give any necessary information. Small craft state their type and say which side they will give way on.

Vessels not navigating by radar in reduced visibility

In conditions of reduced visibility, a single vessel underway sounds one long blast at intervals of not more than one minute. ▬ A convoy sounds two long blasts, at intervals of not more than one minute. ▬ ▬

Any vessel not navigating by radar, on hearing one of those signals apparently forward of its beam, should reduce speed to the minimum at which it can hold its course and navigate with extreme caution. If necessary it should stop or turn.

On Class 1 waterways, any vessel which is not navigating by radar must, on hearing a tritonal signal, take action to avoid collision. If it is near to a bank it should keep close to that bank and, if necessary, stop there until the other vessel has passed. If it is in the channel, especially if it is crossing the channel, it must get clear as quickly as possible.

▬ ▬ ▬ ▬ ▬ On Class 2 waterways, ferries not navigating by radar sound one long blast followed by four short blasts at intervals of not more than one minute.

Supplementary buoys for navigation by radar

Additional markings for navigation by radar are often placed downstream and upstream from bridge piers. They may be yellow floats with radar reflectors on poles.

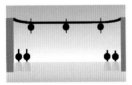

Radar reflectors for overhead cable may be on the cable, giving a radar image of a series of points (not less than 50 metres apart) to identify the cable.

Alternatively, they may be on paired yellow floats below the cable, with each pair giving a radar image of 2 side by side points to identify the cable.

BUOYS MARKING CHANNEL LIMITS IN THE WATERWAY

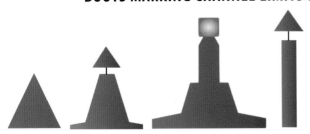

Left hand side of channel
Colour: Green
Form: Conical buoy, or buoy/spar with conical topmark.
Light (if fitted): Rhythmic green.
Often with radar reflector.

Right hand side of channel

Colour: Red
Form: Cylindrical buoy, or buoy/spar with cylindrical topmark.
Light (if fitted): Rhythmic red.
Often with radar reflector.

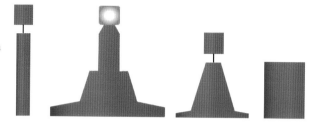

Bifurcation of the channel

Colour: Red and green horizontal bands.
Form: Spherical, or buoy/spar with spherical topmark.
Light (if fitted): Continuous quick, or isophase, or group flashing (3) white.
Often with radar reflector.

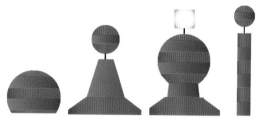

Main channel indicator

A red cylindrical, or green conical topmark may be fitted above the bifurcation buoy to indicate the side on which it is preferable to pass. A rhythmic red or green light as appropriate is fitted.

When a green or red buoy bears a white letter P the channel is next to a berthing area. If a light is fitted to such a buoy its rhythm is different from other buoys indicating the channel limit.

LANDMARKS

Channel is close to left bank.

Channel is close to right bank.

OBSTACLE MARKS

Obstacles on left hand side of channel.

Obstacles on right hand side of channel.

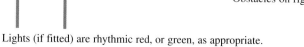

Lights (if fitted) are rhythmic red, or green, as appropriate.

OBSTACLE MARKS (CONTINUED)

 Bifurcation obstacle marks have red and green topmark cones on a post. Light (if fitted) is continuous quick, or isophase, or group flashing (3) white.

Bank walls on approaches to waterway mouths, secondary branches and harbour entrances are often marked, as far as the head of the dividing mole, by obstacle marks.

On the Rhine and certain other navigations, obstacle marks are used to mark the channel and obstacles near the channel. The signs illustrated under 'Landmarks' are not used.

Supplementary obstacle marks

 Spar buoys – red/white on right, green/white on left – may supplement landmarks, for channels near banks, at important obstructions or especially hazardous points. Lights (when fitted) are rhythmic red on right, rhythmic green on left. Spars usually have a radar reflector.

HARBOUR ENTRANCES

The entrance to a harbour is marked by red device to port of a vessel entering and green device to starboard of a vessel entering.

 Port hand marks are generally cylindrical, or a post with a red cylindrical topmark, or a red rectangle painted on a wall.

Starboard hand marks are generally conical, or a post with a conical topmark, or a green triangle painted on a wall.

NOTE: Traffic entering harbours is considered to be going upstream.

CROSS-OVERS

Yellow, or yellow and black, signs are used to mark channel cross-overs. Lights (when fitted) are yellow: flashing group (2) or occulting with even number characteristics on the right bank; flashing group (3) or occulting with odd number characteristics on the left bank.

Signs on right bank, indicating that the channel crosses over to the left bank.

 or Signs on left bank, indicating that the channel crosses over to the right bank.